I Want to Go
in Motion

I Want to Go
in Motion

Poems 1994 - 2018

BOB FOSTER

CONFLUX PRESS · MARINA DEL REY

ACKNOWLEDGMENTS:
Many of these poems have appeared, some in altered
form, in the following publications:
Aethelon
Beyond Baroque Anthology
Creative Living
Ohio State Review
Oxynem
Pentameter
Rose
Spillway
Word Clips
Wordtrack

Cover photograph: *A peaceful sunrise from the ocean
off Fire Island, New York,* by Ron Walker www.rjwphotony.com

Author photograph: Claudia Kunin
Cover and book design: Tania Baban
Printed in the United States of America

ISBN: 978-1-7321123-3-9

CONFLUX PRESS
Marina del Rey, California
www.confluxpress.com

To Paula & Joan

TABLE OF CONTENTS

To a Cherrystone Clam

Rounded blade firmly inserted,
gently I pry your shell open, salivate
at your innocent body,
moist, slippery.

Mouth to edge,
I suck you in whole and alive,
tongue you in circles for a whirl of ambrosia.

A gulp of Adam's apple
and you're swallowed whole, unchewed:
Nude Descending Esophagus.

What is left for us now?
My wish is to lick to a polished gleam
your inner shell

that I was the first to open.

Vintage

His hair too red on white.
Boutonnière blazer
black and white shoes
past row on row
in the vintage car museum.

Studies each
through double-thick lenses.
Smiles
at sign that reads Do Not Touch.
Leans on a creamy
Stutz two-seater.
Peers in a Packard
lined with leather.
Pats serpentine fender
of a black Pierce Arrow
as pairs of eyes
disapprove.

Hop-skips over to an
auburn coupe:
golden tan, canvas top,
celluloid windows.
Slides on in, fakes a key
and mimes ignition
as guards pop up
in the rearview mirror.
He grins,
grips the wheel
stares through walls,
jams pedal to the floor
and roars ahead
down a long, dusty
one-lane road.

Transformation

Shocked
when a bagger at the market
inquires if he can help
with groceries to my car.

Can he see through falling leaves
and peeling bark
to count the circles
in my trunk?

I turn away, my body
bends forward, slimming to fit
the form
of a frail elder

borrowed
from an ancient
Chinese painting.

I shuffle down the parking lot
on dry straw sandals,
pushing an oxcart full of food.

Mirror Flaked With Silver

This nose…a rock,
jutting in silhouette.

Eyes: boiled eggs,
staring from caves.

Forehead, a plaster wall,
seams cracking.

Two weathered gate posts
for frown lines.

A face etched in war,
and love hard-learned.

Barely can see it teenaged,
pressed against cheeks
of grinning schoolgirls.

At our wedding,
a smile
framed with sculpted fears.

The world again in freefall,
something whispers
I should be glad to be visible.

By-Passed

Dropped
spread-eagle
falling
to a river
on fire

On a funeral pyre
shadows
in green
scrub, swab
slice to my heart

Twisted roots
of a riverbank elm
echo a scan
of arteries
blocked

In veil of smoke
a length of vein
pulled from a thigh

is stitched
in place
for blood
to the heart

And the sound:
the sound
is horses
pounding
the earth

Libido, Still

Walking past, very Prada
she turns and smiles
just smiles, like a page in *Vogue*.

Something more than friendly
vibrates my temples
wriggles my vertebrae
tickles the testes of me, back
in my thirties. Free-falls to a
a boy in his teens, thrilled
with the thrust of his first
wet dream

Her smile, an unspoken
invitation to a candlelight dinner
a tango to her bedroom on a
cloud of Berber white.
Feeling like a GQ hunk
until my arthritic knees
slip into unstoppable spasms
Extricating from my favorite
position, she whispers:

"Sorry Pops, but I have an early
morning shoot with Britney on Rodeo.
Call a cab on me."

There to Here

If I fall in the marriage crevasse again
I'll scrape my way out
with the first appearance of cumulonimbus clouds.

Pressed to blame compulsive escapes
on an angsty Stravinsky childhood,
I'll reveal scars of a frontal lobotomy.

Like a butcher-block chicken
pulled inside out, I'm me.

Exposed and easily rattled,
I joyfully labor today in a cocoon of my own making,
sticking curlicue phrases
to hungry blank pages
with thoughts I don't have the chutzpah
to tell the world to its face.

Saltless, Fatless, Meatless

I remember Kansas City Prime,
New York Cut with Beaujolais.
London Broil, sliced on the bias
with blood-red squeeze.

Forkfuls of Garlic Pot Roast,
Cheese and Pepper Sausages,
Turkey dark meat, dripping
golden essence of the bird.

Food was leaves and fruit,
till we swung down from the trees
to track a Rack of Lamb, grope
a Lobster by the tail.

But Wheat Sprout burgers?
Taste-free Tofu? Yolkless Eggs
in yellow dye? Salt is not
to live without, pour it on!

Shovel sugar in the Whipping Cream.
Slime Butter on my toast.
Cholesterol? I'll eat a bowl of it!
Take a knife—cut my heart out—

but cook it, let me eat it, please!

19

An Apparition

Dripping wet sand,
it raised an arm
as if to wave
then backed away
and bulked off
into the black.

Over fireplace drinks
the story told
brings neighbors'
winks
disparaging smiles.

But I'd seen the figures
in their weirdness!

Learned later
what to keep secret
and what to blame
on the fog.

The creatures
in boots, backpacks
and bedrolls
were a Green group
of varied professionals
holding to a previous plan
made in the city to hike
the shoreline
on a glorious weekend
in August.

Shall I Buy the Painted Collage?

Bold green strokes for a storm
off New England. Mountainous waves
with troughs for valleys
straining the saltwater canvas.

Seagulls pinned to the sky by the wind.
Fishing boat yaws on the sides of tip-over canyons.
Half the catch floats in the wake
at the split of dawn.

Follow a broad coast-to-coast palette
of earth tones: wheat to water, snow to desert
and a distant Pacific Blue.

Vanilla-white ferries, slicing through fabric wrinkles,
to sienna humps of strewn-about islands.
Sun-striped homes of the awesome, poised on
the cliffs of maybe. Oil wells costumed as palm trees.
Giant grasshopper-mobiles bobbing for oil assets.
Fish with the heads of sheep.

I can't resist, I'll buy the art and live here!

Frame it myself in white macramé, screw it
to the ceiling over my newly-divorced
permanently single, permanently unmade bed.

Crustacean à la Carte

Bug-eyed but sexy: broiled
New England Lobster
fresh from the wave-splashed
coast of Maine.

Fired bright red
and split down the middle
like an unzipped swimsuit.
Eight slender legs
to suck salt/sweet
with Chardonnay.
Tail twists off
like a turn in tango.
Large claw cracked
and drenched in butter
is softest Breast
of Mermaid.

Sprinkle white flesh with
lemon drop rain
and your tongue has been tickled
by the best of the planet.

Far North

Wide tracks of oversized tires
where caribou fall to give birth,
in shadows of giant rigs that punch
major holes in the slope
for the blackest blood of the planet.

From the seat of the nation,
a message rising on smoke, reflected
in lakes, says reindeer, foxes wolves,
eagles will continue to breed and feed,
and pose for photos, as the white oasis
is trampled and drained, by every form
of steel, wheel, and turbine.

But lovers of nature's music
read every drop of oil on snow
as a note in a requiem, for unique
mountain vistas and thin Arctic gene lines
left hanging in frigid wind.

Unsigned

I lift a grey seascape
   from falling
         surf.
Acrylic paint
    on large wooden
    breadboard
 touches my saline spirit.

Its black ducks in thin lines
    skim whitecaps
      brushed onto splinters.

Abandoned boatmast tossed
       in hostile swells.

In a single bite, breaking wave
          swallows sandcastle
    children labored on half the afternoon.

Atop painted dunes
    in rows of low bleached
  houses, long young faces
    stare through
pimples of morning raindrops.

I Abhor Flowers

trees and plants, whose
exotic scents rise
with allergens
to irritate eyeballs
   nostrils
membranes of the epiglottis
and explode
as nose grenades.
Suspend my life for
five
   six
      seven
sneezes in a row.
Spoiling
sex at the peak
or an afterglow
a smoke
  a wine
     extended touching.

Except my favorite:
the cozy nose-to-neck position
erasing
other allergens
with the scent of her
Chanel.

Birthday Fourteen: a BB Rifle

in crosshairs, a redbreast, swaying on
branch, blurring the focus.

i aim at a sparrow, it hops behind leaf.
i'm back to the robin, ready to fly. but
finger on trigger is hardly mine, when it
jerks, fires, holds me enthralled as the

bird drops through fall leaves to dry grass;.
eyes half-open in death; wing bloody red
as its chest. I'm nearly fainting, guilty of
killing a god-made creature of song.

no reason but a scary new sense of power
that I might brag of to friends, but what

to tell ma? *What to tell her?* dollars for
food, spent on an executioner?

My Inner Fish

First, buy a fish,
a large Tuna. Dress it up
as a two-legged walking mammal: me,
after three million years
>of swimming, crawling, eating leaves
>in a hair suit. All before
my running leap to less hair, bigger brains
and thumbs I can twiddle.

>I revel in feeling fishy,
>breathing through jaws and ears,
>flip-flopping my tail down rainy streets
>finning around in pet shops
>blinking at family in watery prisons.

Their ancestors all grew bones for my hands,
knees, wrists and arms. Plus other basic stuff for cells
and human organs.

>If my aroma is too salt or briny,
>please forgive, for I would never, never,
>as some might wish, reject the source,
>my inner fish.

Wish I'd Been

a Beat Poet in the Venice West of the '60s,
with bald head or brillo for hair,
I'd have joined in an upswell of poets,
passionate artists who saw poetry not just as art
but as weapon.

Their banner: Down with Authority; wrote a thunder of poems
for underground journals and tabloids: antiwar, antilaw,
poems for peace, freedom, drugs.

Poets of the Gas House Restaurant,
expresso joints on what became Abott Kinney,
swigs of wine swallowed "in secret" at no-booze tables,
they'd write sober and edit drunk,
short and long, beyond the margins up the side of the page,
with the chewed ends of number two pencils.
Real poets, wannabe poets, star poets.

Wanda Coleman bombarded walls—
"Riots? Yes! I write from the riots inside me!"

Jack Hirshman lived on a platform in trees—
"Dumpsters, alleys littered with discarded human crumbles;
panhandlers at corners, along walls…"

Charles Bukowski's poems didn't sell
until German critics wrote,
"Ausgezeichnet, dieser Mann is ein Genie!"—
"The days here are like wild horses running away."

Clair Horner wrote in abandoned cars and called his book
Don't Step on the Bacon, Man!—
"A poem a day keeps the psychiatrist away? Not my kind!"

Frances Dean Smith renamed herself "FrancEyE,"
she wrote to find out who she was—
"When a man asked why I grew a chin beard,
I told him I am a wise woman."

Philomene Long and John Thomas wrote poems to people in jail:
"We open a door. There is no road. We take it."

Wish I'd been like them, with their
fusion of anger and art and madness.
They gave their readers a kick in the rear.
Wish I'd been one of them.

Hallucinations on an African Hunt

From the tall grass, barely seen
the leopardess snarls at the hunter,
growls that she is predator not prey.
"You prissy, girly-boy tracker
of my mating scent!"

As he peers through brush, his rifle wilts.

"Make your move," she snorts,
"I'll pull you down for buzzards to eat,
rip out the walls of your heart."

"Smartass!" he counters.
"Tall grass pussycat!"

She hisses. Spots move. A single eye
slides behind a leaf, re-appears as she
leaps into the clearing,
revels in her flaunting mode:
"Drop that limp old Remington,
all you want is overnight sluts,
but I'm hunting a legal lifetime samesex mate!

"I'll take a nap in the crotch of that tree,"
she goes on. "You can snore on worms and ants.
Early in the dawn while I'm hunting love,
if another whiff of estrus is hanging in the air,
follow it: deep in the green
could lie a female crocodile
that hasn't had a man in years!"

A Dictionary Alice

A bird, a phosphamedon bird,
circles,
stops midflight,
dances a rustiform slurry.

Dives like a candycane arrow
at kewpy doll eyes in a scrupulous desert.

Califactorious claws, hook into the flesh
of a screeching, wriggling quagga,
impaled on its dangling fosdic.

Six quick pecks and the mess is enormous,
all lictorial libers, finger food for the leucotome ants.

No Punch and Judy about it,
this is a world of Talleyrand wings,
headwaiter harmattans,

and end-of-the-species lunar rovers,
bones in place, no need to dig up.

I'll record them all
on quadri-syllabic, multi-canopic videotape.
Distribute them gratis

to pseudo-phrenologists, Oedipus-ologists
bandana banana parapsychologists.

Plus a drink
to my one undecillion
Alice.

Early Kodak Album

Like a cornstalk alongside a pumpkin,
the Foster twins Henry and Howard appear
to have come from planets apart.
Howard cried louder at birth; maybe a lawyer
or an auctioneer.

Still sucking his thumb at fourteen,
Henry
morphed to this smiling driver
of black limousines.
Red wine under his seat, saved for later,
swallowed like water.

Howard, sober, sold classified ads for the *Post*,
first in family to own a car.
Sundays he'd drive us in circles around the block,
with canvas top down, to the waves and whoops
of our Irish neighbors, crowding out of church.

Frank, the oldest, worked too hard,
died too young, left a trickle of tears
from a pregnant girlfriend. And former wife
shouting in Spanish for a slice of insurance
to feed her boys on the West Coast.

Sister Roberta married rich old men. Lived high
    on vodka and gilt-edged bonds,
dressed here, for a cigar-smoking party
    in newest nightclub regalia,
with custom-tailored bearded lover from Osaka.

    And there's Ma and Pa at twenty years
        mismatched.
I hated it when the kids next door
    would call them
    Mr. Drunk and Mrs. Sober.

Skippy

I named her Skippy, for the spaces skipped on
her brown, black and white little mixed-breed
face. Her tail, an all-black spinning propeller,
with white paws perfect for skidding on linoleum
floors. I was nine years old, and didn't like girls,
but when Pa called Skippy a bitch, I got mad and
kissed her nose like she was my baby sister. A
neighbor said I was in love with Skippy. We hardly
used that word in our family. I just knew she
was all I thought of, how she learned to smile and
dance two-legged with me for her treats. Once,
she got stuck back-to-back mating with a big
German shepherd, so I hosed him with water
till he took off. But Skippy looked like she wasn't
quite sure I'd done the right thing. When her
puppies came, I felt like their uncle. She let me
lift them and show them before anyone else.
Then, about one year later, it happened: she
ran outdoors, got run over and killed by a
baker's truck. But...I just can't write about that
anymore.

Questions for Leah

Is your crimson hair now cloud white?
Have you mothered a trio
of swan-like daughters
or, like me, shuffled
through the waltzes of life mostly alone?

A half century later,
are you still as uncertain as when we
undressed at fifteen,
forehead to forehead,
fumbling with buttons
in oak leaf shadows?

The shock
of you standing half-clothed
then flying off
like a winged silhouette,
robbing us both of the thigh-to-thigh
and chest-to-breast
long promised!

Was it that maybe
you lost the urge
to take the leap with a boy
trembling more than you?

Momma

After Pa stomped away to work
each day, she'd squeak our bedroom doors
to wake us for school.

On weekends, I'd stand shyly by
as she'd smile her very best smile
at the butcher, pat the cheese man's cheek,
open her hazel eyes real wide and ask
Mr. Fruit and Produce
if she could squeeze his plums.

Sister once whispered that she saw Momma
drink beer with Mr. Sadoff,
and kiss him, right there in our kitchen.
I snarled at her and she said she was lying.
He sold boy's clothing
door-to-door, once left a free
pair of socks for me.
Momma said it was just because he liked me.

Miss Katrina Verning

Jogging through rain-flecked leaves
her chest rose up, fell back, rose up, fell back.
I tried to stare at her hazel eyes
and full lips, but her long damp skirt hugged
        soft lengths of thigh
        with every lunge.

On this chill damp night in Boston, to me, age 9,
    she was a pretty German immigrant girl
        of 17, just off the boat.
    Miss Katrina Verning.
The rest of the time she was my mother.

Once, at the Gardner Museum, her face
    appeared to me in a painting
of a woman lying naked on purple grass.
        After half an hour of staring
    a guard moved me on.

"This is the good clean life," Ma said,
her breath steaming past neighborhood street lamps
        on that spring evening.

I dreaded curving the puddled road home,
    where she slept with my drunken Pa.
The sight of him dissolved me
    to a mound of boy's clothing

        to be sink-washed and hung out to dry
        on a clothesline

in Katrina *Foster's* hands.

Ma

For eight months, floating in her fluid,
I am bumped, turned on my side nearly upside-down.
It's Pa, drunk, trying to have sex with her
when she would have none of it.
She crosses her legs at the knees, and locks them so tight
that with all his strength he cannot pry them
apart. As her thirteenth fetus,
I have recently learned from her whispered words,
the deep purpose of her fierceness is to inform him
that once I have left the birth canal, she will
never become pregnant by him again.

A silence, then a thump, as one of them falls
from bed to floor; must be Pa.
I'm yanked forward and squeezed between them, as he pulls her
down on top. Then I'm flung against the wall
of her womb as she staggers up, runs to the bathroom,
slams the door, bolts it against him.
When he pounds on it, I shake like the doorknob
and hold onto my cord as he shouts
"Katie! Katie! Open up!"

Rough Couplets

Popping up like a sudden iceberg among family
photos, the face of our marmalade cat startled

me as though calling up the total scenes of my
childhood all at once, and with great pain:

There was Pa, throwing a plateful of hot spaghetti
at the cat I loved but he called Evil Spirit.

She would leap away leap screaming as if on fire,
and I also suffered the loss of a second dish of pasta.

Saturdays at the Strand

So packed with kids we had to sit up
on the hardwood stage, no chairs
and way off to each side of the screen.
Picture so close and view so slanted
Hopalong's hat took on the look of a
squeeze-up tent. The villain's mustache
stretched out past his shoulders, angled
face of the rancher's daughter
appeared like a tilted billboard.

A Baby Ruth
  was passed among us
    as leaning-left
      sheriffs chased
        leaning-right bandits
          through
            sideways gullies
              up too-tall mountains
                down shoelace trails
                  to the scrunched-up
                    city of Dodge.

In the almost-kissing scene, we
squirmed at the full-screen lips,
and as Hoppy rode off in a zigzag
sunset, the chandeliers bloomed.
We cheered, clapped and rubbed
the sage dust from our eyes.
And to a boy, agreed he was right
in leaving that mascaraed cowgirl:
dark-shadowed eyes, and dyed
blond hair cascading down from
her off-kilter head.

A Conversion

Protestant boy, squeezed between half-asleep Joey Kelly
and a freckled Mickey O'Brien, in the Catholic Church
of the Precious Blood, awed by the pageantry in gold, purple,
Irish-accented Latin prayers, basins of water
for spilling on newborn babies, altars of streaked Italian marble
where parishioners knelt for blood-of-Christ wine and wafers
as great organ chords strike at their souls.
To a ninety-pound weakling, it felt like the Power I'd prayed for.

Nightly dreams of decades ahead in a round white collar
serenely dispensing forgiveness to
thieves, sexpots, cardinal sinners,
some with no idea why they were there.
To test the Catholic faith, I attended a synagogue,
a Buddhist temple and
a storefront wreck called Love Big Daddy.
Easily Catholics won out,
and at sixteen up to my hips in the Precious Blood
I converted, with thoughts of a Seminary enrollment.
But, facing lifelong abstinence,
I instead trained to lead the choir.
My father and siblings finally accepted my conversion.
Only my haloed mother, Katherine, fiercely declined, yet agreed
I could address her, from then on, as Mary.

Ma, Pa, Me

In ancient black and white photo
Pa, half-drunk, wears old grey
   winter suit to a sunny beach
      in July.
   His head a puff of dandelion hair,
he stares at Ma
   who tries to smile:

Through cracked, creased
   picture surface,
      I ask
"Why did you tear Jesus
   from around your neck
      and kick him into the sewer
   as you waited for my Sunday class to end?"

But, in a golden moment,
 you also raced across
   a junk-filled lot to lift me
from stones when I'd fallen
      hard
   from a tree.
   Held me so close
I was part of your body.
A first, brief awareness
   of what must have been love.

Next breath,
    see a lovely timid young
    German girl,
        you, looming up behind,
ready to cheat her
    of a church-and-flowers wedding,
    inflating her womb
    thirteen times.

    Yet, at your funeral,
when she brushed hair from your forehead,
    I shook with the memory
        of deep
    in your arms.

"Get Him Out of My Kitchen, Robert!"

Brushing past, Ma leaves me alone
with Pa, drunk in long-johns stained yellow.
He stands defiant in my face,
arms held up like a boxer.

I'm fifteen and scared.
For a slice of a second the world goes black.
My eyes open to blood on his lips,
his face twisted to a question mark.

My knuckles red, but no memory
of making a fist, swinging my arm, or any impact.
Lifting that hand, I motion him
out of the kitchen.

He stares, then says, "Sure, sock your old man,
like all your brothers." Then turns, shuffles away
to his separate bedroom, wiping blood.
My arms feel like lead.

Next day, dressed for Boston High School,
I walk into the kitchen where Ma sits
sipping tea, looking tired.
She smiles, rises with open arms, we hug—too long,

kiss—too long, before she backs away, dabs
at her eyes, looks out the window.
I stand rooted,
mind revolving, body sparked.

22 Hancock Street, Boston

Four-story wooden tenement:
diapers would soak in metal washtubs,
the smell of booze heavy on my old man's breath.

Now an empty lot, but surrounding buildings
                still stand, as in a dream
        of early childhood.
Brighter colors, like an old photo,
         retouched.

The battered movie house now books
rock bands. Nickel Candy Store
          no more,
         laptop repairs instead.

I still see chocolate wafers
      on a cut-glass stand, encircled by
             sugared greenleaves,
lollipops, chocolate caramels,
                 almond creams.

And a boy without a coin.

Tell Me With Your Eyes

Naked together, under her family porch.
From between floorboards
slants of light stripe us.

I'm fourteen, pale, skinny,
aroused by Mary Guest, thirteen.
Blond hair, sunburned skin
to her small white red-dot breasts.

Transfixed by hair
in her valley of thighs
I can't believe she just takes my hand,
places it there, shuts her eyes.

Birdsongs! Love! In a bower
of tropical leaves, we're pressing
thighs that begin to tremble, like
longstem lilies in pelting rain.

Shouts and gunshots! Bootsteps
shake the jungle floor. Mary's dad,
dressed for a safari, stares at me
like searchlight beams.

A single stroke of his shiny machete
and my severed head falls to Mary's lap,
plants a kiss on her belly.
"He's a lover!" someone shouts.

I pray Mary heard the grandeur
in those words, and will tell me so
with her eyes, when next we meet
in Reptile Reproduction Class.

Locked In

If I leave my mother's kitchen
she'll feel alone in her war against my father.
The smell of her baking helps me to stay.

I'm always hungry, he's always drunk.

On the papered wall
above the kitchen table
there's a printed yellow tree
she washes every day.
But a spot of red near the knothole
shows we ate spaghetti last night.

One kitchen chair has been mine
since the age of six.
"That's Robert's chair,"
my mother tells the others
including my glassy-eyed father.

Hot water pipes
knock-thump-rattle across the ceiling
when my mother runs too much hot
for boiling chicken, or soaking beans
for her Saturday Special.

Baked beans and sausage or hot dogs
every Saturday night of our lives.
My dog Skippy isn't allowed in the kitchen,
I hide her behind the garbage can,
secretly flip her scraps of meat.
She knows to stay quiet
or she'll be chased away with a broom.

Between meals, across our kitchen window,
a bedroom in the house next door:
Irish newlyweds—were my parents ever that wild?
I can't believe Catholics behave that way
with the shade up, the lights on!

Howard (A Father I Wished For)

Short, with sickly skin, pale green eyes
made smaller by double-thick lenses.
Older brother.

Howard was a mind on edge,
a heart on course
for a life I believed
he could paint any color he dreamed.
Except for a sulfurous breath,
never cured.

Wore a suit, a shirt and tie
to sell classified ads for the *Boston Herald*.
Bought a topdown old Buick,
drove us around and around the block
to cheers and applause
from Irish and Italian neighbors.
A quarter of a century later he cheered for me
when credits rolled on TV shows
with my name!

Called the day before he died,
coughed *I love you, Bob,
you're shootin' high and I love it.*

Bob and *love.*
Words I never heard from my father.

Between Snowfalls

Leafless trees
spray frost on windows,
last week's fall
in patches.
Shivering to junior high
past homes like ads in magazines,
with fireplace, electric heat. Ripe tomatoes
and asparagus in winter
on dinner plates that match.

Fourth floor walkup flat,
linoleum floors, and seven
sprouting children on a single weekly paycheck.

I'll want a house, a car,
a wife with permanent wave.
Then there's this gift my mother talks of.
Not wrapped in a box
but a mysterious thing God gave to me
at birth, she says. Someday you'll know, son,
and you'll be like no one else in the world.

It crowds out history and algebra
this January morning
my nose dripping
boots crunching ice,
another snow
waiting to fall.

Man to Man in Boston

Mother moaning through their bedroom door,
I couldn't hear the doctor, or what
my father mumbled.
I was scared that she would die
and he would be in charge.

Two days later she was up, cooking.
He, almost drunk, staring at me reading
in the living room. Leaning forward,
he spoke slowly, You would have had—
another sister—if it hadn't dropped on out
before its time.

At only ten, I caught his meaning,
not just from the words but his expression;
like reaching his arms to me through his eyes.
It was as though he was someone else's father
telling his son a family secret.

And would I ever see that look again?

1920: At the Bottom of the Silent Screen*

Softly, the dark flutes of Autumn sound in the reeds.

The Columbine removes her clothes,
delights at her reflection in the pond.

Two white roses strike the water;
she runs to the harboring trees.

A man, whose body casts two shadows,
appears, and speaks:

> *You are perfumes in a silent night.*
> *Rise up and live with me*
> *an inch above that star.*

My mind confuses which star,
but I see in your eyes an intention.

> *I will live in you,*
> *and where you are empty*
> *I will build a roadway of lightning.*

So many words to believe, that come
only from the round of your lips.

> *Where light invades the night of the heart*
> *we will consummate love*
> *and sleep like wine in goblets.*

But I have lived apart from those carnal rites.

> *You must of course lie on your back*
> *and let yourself drift:*
> *I will be your guide.*

The Columbine sighs, smiles, closes her eyes.

 A cento

Big Brother Frank

Half-smothered in layers of steaming burlap, a large figure
rises as though from the River Styx, at the Ford plant near
Boston. Among bangs, roars and screeches of machine-
on-machine, he is hosed down with ice-cold water four
minutes of every hour, to drop his one-hundred-two-
degrees back to normal. His skin bleached like a boiled
potato, blue eyes red as beets, he is my oldest brother,
Frank, twenty-six. Back in the pit, only a handkerchief
for a face mask, he resumes spraying boiling hot rust-proof
paint on the undersides of new cars. Nine-hour days,
six-day weeks, he grinds away at this job, helping to keep
our family of seven in clothes, food and AM radio.

Weeknights he comes home after dark, eats a meal our
mother keeps warm, and drops into bed, exhausted.
But Saturday nights, after a bath and dinner of home-
baked beans, he lifts all fifty-three pounds of me on his
bare shoulders and we march up the hall to our partly-
furnished parlor. Smiling, with his thick left arm held out
for me to hold on, he asks "Ready?" "Yup" I answer, and
his deep singing voice fills the room with the thumping
music of a merry-go-round. He'll swing me in circles,
round and round, faster and faster in a blur of windows
and doors, until that time he starts squinting and looking
dizzy and slows down so I can let go of his arm.

Both sweating, we wipe each other's faces with dish towels and fan ourselves with pieces of cardboard box. He gulps down a couple of aspirins from his shirt pocket and says, "Don't tell anyone about this Bobby, it's nothin' and it's gonna go away. Let's do some more merry-go-round!" But he looks tired. It's getting close to my study time and I want him to hear the new story I made up about a friendly robot who slams, twists and bolts a whole new car together by himself, every day, at a plant on the moon. But Frank is too sleepy and goes to bed.

Exactly forty-two days later, in the loud machine wilderness of Ford, the dizziness hit him again. They told me that at first he just stood straight up, then began to sway, dropped his spray-gun and fell over dead in the pit. I asked if I could have a sheet of his initialed burlap wetcloth, and they gave it to me.

The Robert/Roberta Diary Notes

I'm only fifteen
but I am the baby's uncle.
She's named for me, only a bedroom
wall between us.

I change, wash, and spoon her now.
She burps with a giggle, makes poops
with a grin. So much of me in her eyes,
hair, and quickness.

I mimic her grandpa and animals,
and she applauds at all the right places.
Neighbors call me a sissy, and my beagle
Skippy recently squeezed out an extra litter,
hoping to win me back.

When Roberta's sea-going father returns
to cuddle his daughter, she holds to her mother,
or reaches out crying for me.
We calm her with rocking, then gingerly
pass her to him.

On Thanksgiving Day I stepped each step
of her very first walk. Now she stands alone
and crosses the room like a wind-up toy.

Today, my life has taken a tilt.
Her parents are moving to a flat of their own,
twenty-two bus miles away,
and I'll have to stay here with my folks.

She left this afternoon, face so red,
pouting with tears.

I'll try not to look in her bedroom tonight.

Interlude: A Romance

At first light
she walks the fall beach
in a winter coat,
denting the sand so lightly.

At sunrise, gone;
through a cut in the dunes.
Late afternoon, reappears
on the boardwalk.
I speak, she pauses.
Turns full-face.
Her eyes seductive.

     Approaches the deck
     of my fisherman's shack,
     we share fruit, cheese,
     chocolate chip cookies.
     Parts her lips only to eat.
     And those eyes!
     Shall I take her tan face
     in my hands
     or will she frighten away,
     disappear again?

The food gone, I follow as she walks
to a stand of blue pines,
refuses a kiss to her forehead,
vanishes through needled branches.
Leaving me to await her return in spring,
feeding on newly-green leaves
with her own, newly-born, spotted fawn.

Jeanine Is Leaving

Puzzled, annoyed,
fishing the surf,
he casts the lure
out on the cold
October ocean.
Teases it along the waves,
like a crippled sardine.
Dances it on the bottom
like a shrimp
in the throes of death.
Hooks nothing
but scenes of Jeanine
packing, writing him a note,
starting her car.

Cold salt spray
tenses his skin
as another cast reels in only
flashes of his runaway lover
driving the bridge
to Alternate South.
Higher waves
nearly knock him over
until, rod on shoulder,
he trudges downbeach
to his weathered house on the dune.

Project in Process

The stretched mound bulges.
Grunts and groans from the first-time momma,
perspiration from the first-time Dad.

Deep inside, the Project tilts,
awaits her launch.
Pushed down hard,
squeezed out dripping
like a parboiled chicken.
Feedline trailing
from the burned-out Mom,
Daddy in a heap on the green tile floor.

Upside down and whacked on the bottom,
the Thing inflates,
turns purple-red.
Transmogrifies
to a wriggling, squint-eyed
all-out daughter
with prehistoric spark in bright new brain,
a meteor shower of pizzazz.

Ma Remembered

Side-to-side,
    across her chest I'm baby-rocked
    staring up at her face.
I'm sleepy from endless pendulum swings
         my eyes never off hers.
Tears
    wet her blouse, dropping me off
      at kindergarten
as Boston Irish neighbors smirk
      at her German accent.

Siblings later would always complain:

You were her favorite!
We saw it, heard it,
we were jealous but quiet.
You never played with any of us,
you took up sewing,
peeled carrots and potatoes,
the sissy-boy of the family!

I just stare at her picture…

Mileage

Spinning, spinning,
adding miles to a storm of emotion
over our Boston flat, born of anger in our
immigrant German mother, stuck with seven
kids and hardly a sober husband.
Add miles of chord for bonding me to her
in my teens; me with no understanding
of why she wanted me close.

Uphill driving for many more miles
before she would loosen the chord
enough for me to risk a local drive
with a schoolgirl my age. Then she freed up
her grip again, permitting kisses, but no falling
in love. That, she claimed, could be controlled,
like mileage on the odometer.

Miles further down the highway, by the time
of her funeral,
I had never lived with, faked the game with,
or had more than overnighters with women.
Marriages mostly resembled the car crash
I grew up in. Until Jane.

She shook my chassis, stopped my speedometer,
ejected hung-over memories of primal disasters
in the cocoon. I dreamt of bumper stickers shouting,
Honk For This To Work
Jane, an actress; gorgeous, bright, talented; a person
I could try the Real Road with, unafraid.

I lied. Lied to myself, to Jane, and to the worldwide
parking lot. Nothing I tried could transform me into
a person free of the bond in my childhood.

Returned From Paris Undelivered, 1917*

Announced by trumpets of smoke
I parachute into a field of dangers.
Fire and ether rush through my veins,
my back aches as if all the vertebrae
have been cracked open.

Carried through rooms of fear
in a farmhouse, I see insects
peer down from villages in the molding.
When fed, I feel the thrum of war
in the round of a spoon.

And a shiver of branches in the trees
of my heart. But even in pain, on this
failed day of our wounded Republic,
I long for your voice that never fades,
even with the ocean turned up high.

*A cento inspired by French poems of World War I.

Naked

Depressed on my fiftieth birthday.
A millionare I'm certainly not, nor a movie star
nor a famous/infamous dealer in drugs.
Lucky star needs a laser beam.

Only "good morning" from Gloria
and the kids. They had forgotten the date.

Greeted at the office by
loyal Janice. "Good Morning Sir, and Happy Birth-
day!"
I felt grateful, half my age and moon-
struck, though this Bluebell blossom
claimed a devotion to worklife platonic.

At her invitation to lunch, I zoomed back
to age nineteen, my eyes glued to the steam
of a hot Brazilian stripper sliding the pole.

Margaritas and cucumber sandwiches
and with a smile that embraced the whole northeast
she suggested we stop at her apartment. In a
snowfall of ladies' panties, I became sixteen, with
a permanent crease in the crotch of my pants.
"Make yourself comfy," she said, slinking into her
bedroom. Now I'm fourteen, awaiting my first
no hands, daytime nocturnal emission.

Minutes passed as months until she returned
in an exploding rush with Gloria and the children
shouting birthday greetings,
waving bow-tied presents.

I sat there, head in hands, unavoidably nude
totally unscrewed, watching my children
screw up their faces with, "That's what Daddy
looks like naked!?"

Then eight a.m. rang out.

At Her Bedside

Are you my brother, or my uncle? Do you live with us?
Is this my house? That woman in the room won't let me
sleep, she sings off-key and tells me to shut up.

I have to use the bathroom, call a nurse. I want
the little black one, her hands aren't cold.

Will you be here when I get back? You weren't always nice
to me when we were children, but, you see, I cry as
I look at you now. Don't go away.

Two Minus One

A green world igniting again
to copper, crimson, yellow:
our favorite view through
the large picture window
installed to celebrate
our matching rings.

I think of the comfort we felt
with new friends in Amsterdam last winter.
And the amazement of that Kenyan family
when we explained our married status!

But, George, I'm lost since you quietly died
out there on the porch
in your wicker chair.
I plod the hours through a blur
of darks and daylights.

My nephew keeps asking: "Uncle Tim,
is George still happy
being with God?"

Some days I wish I had the courage
to use a chemical passport to join you.

Discovered in the Snows of Peru

An Inca girl in a rock-pile hut
high in the Andes
dressed this day in a cloth of silver

a chanting a drumming
a ringing of bells
by her mother and aunts

Did she know? Or was she drugged
and told she'd be a princess?

a chanting a drumming
a ringing of bells
by sisters and uncles

Higher in the snow of the Cordillera
silver cloth is removed by her father

a chanting a drumming
a ringing of bells
by the holy priest

Were her eyes shut tight
or forced wide open
as her skull was crushed
by rock in the hands of the holy one?

See her parents' pride in gifting the gods
with virgin sex, for hopeful harvest

five hundred years
to her shrunken face
two dark holes staring from snow

At the Edge

A slit of pink
    cuts through
        grey dawn horizon.

The ocean blinks
    with waves
        and troughs.

Splashings of lace
    fall into foam
        climb the dry beach

where my
    shadow
        begins

Bluefish Bay: Fog

Pale hints   of small boats
    anchored   rocking

a gull glides through—
    melts back in

a distant chugging
    turns   dwindles

my rain suit
      rustles

metal fish lure—
    clicks against the rod

waves lap at algae
       on a buoy

louder
    than the damped moan
    of foghorn

Whippersnapper Daughter

Head of a circus horse,
brown-and-white, appears in a leaded glass
window, snorts steam from under
its jeweled bridle. Moves aside, reveals a group
of performing horses, munching on mounds
of pink cotton candy.

In a flash of sunset,
all white horses morph into orange
or silhouette black. At the snap of a whip
they freeze in position and stare at an
intense young woman, silver booted in a green
top hat. She snaps again and the
brown-and-white on tense hind legs,
dances to tango in a sawdust ring, nods the
quick rhythms of bluegrass strings,
then bows to its trainer; her long blue
whip laid aside.

As audience applauds
the grey-haired Master Of Rings
her father drops to one knee,
kisses her hand, grins up at a face
he's adored since her birth.

Through a Knothole at a Summer Cottage

Close-up view   a blade of grass   bent by a beetle
legging its way to drink from a dewdrop
at far end of a bushy tunnel a cow tugs hard at a fat red worm
the worm will not give up without splitting apart
crouching nearby   a field mouse locked in fear of a bird
until all-of-a-quickness it flickers its nose   bristles its fur
races away   vanishing into the forest of stems
risking a splinter I press my brow against the knothole
for a wider view including the sundeck of a neighbor's house
where the screen door opens and a little girl bursts out
in a swimsuit giggling   running   followed by a doting father
the mother reads by the pool   she looks up smiling
father and daughter seem to be shrinking
but return around the other side   now they're large as life
they crowd the knothole with faces of none other than
myself and daughter   in this daydream of un-divorce

Mess

Mounds of mail,
spreads of coins.
Afraid to lift an envelope.
That something underneath
will leap awake,
bite my mind.
Rent overdue.
Shutting off the power.
Another notice from the bank.

Cleaning lady quit twice
in different languages.

But, at the bottom of the pile,
scent of gardenia
from the widow of a friend!
On vacation in Hawaii
changing planes at LAX
and would like to spend
a night or two!

Dated December a year ago.

South of Point Conception

A seacliff high, of yellow shale and darker layers
crunched into place under billions of tons, eons
of sabertooth tigers, prehistoric wolves, wooly mammoths.

I lean the cliff, to hear echoes of fossils swimming the rock.
On ledges below, shallow pools
the ocean keeps full for fossils-to-be.

Against sky, pelicans out of dinosaurs, glide, dive,
crash the water to fish for life. On a beach, sea lions
shimmy a train in sand to the ocean's edge,

drop deep into forests of kelp, where mackerel, bonita and perch
try to escape. One wave, larger than others,
shudders the beach, and I breathe a mist

of bubbles popping in foam. On land behind the cliff
mile after mile of red-orange rooftops, endless ribbons
of anywhere/everywhere freeways—

discouraging signs for animals, plants, nesting birds
and swirling creatures that could have left further records of life,
in a last ocean cliff, on the last solid land.

Starting Over Alone

Half-drawn shades, raindrops on panes.

Walls freshly painted, not even room for books in boxes.

Shirts hanging from shiny doorknobs to slippery bare floors.

Laptop on volume of Shakespeare's *Kings.*

Bag of old laundry in new kitchen closet.

Bronze head of ex-wife not yet returned.

Daughter at twelve riding blue-ribbon horse.

Beachscape painting, time waits for tide to erase:

> *Paula, Mom, Dad* fingered in sand.

Rash

In fall, voluptuous vine
of leaves circus-colored
obscures the skeleton
of white birch tree it has strangled
top to bottom.

Backlit in October sun
each boldly-colored leaf displays
arteries and veins
like the human heart.

But they are heartless:
will split your skin
with open sores
and running pus

with a touch
as light
as butterfly wing.

Harry

Sober, hanging in on his thirty-footer
cradled in winter boatyard. Space heater,
port-a-john; a builder out of business.

Ginger Ale in topless bars,
DVD's of cops and killers,
thirteen months alone.

Yearning for something warm and carnal
with the waitress at the diner,
hair streaked grey exactly like his ex's.

He leaves tips beyond his means
in hopes she won't refuse a call
from under a Navajo blanket
some cloud-white Sunday night

after his alternate-weekend daughters
have gone back home.

Forty-Three Degrees in April

Thwacks of the hatchet
as kindling drops
plink-and-plunk in driftwood notes.

A match scratched to old news
snuffed in the woodstove
waltzes the fire
into yellow silk scarves,
swirling, encircling, devouring
the wood for my comfort.

Outside
a chilled world of tight buds
hugging twigs, spaces for green
waiting for cues
from deep in the solar heating system.

Mid-April

pours down from bucketed clouds,
soaks the new roof, ricochets from doors
to porch in a clap of cannons and staggered flashes.
Under dry eaves, orange-red robins
and sly sparrows away from their nests
blink in sync with liquid knuckles
knocking on windows, splitting the ground,
splashing mud on Bayberry blooms to unfold
their petals into fragile dams that quickly fill
and burst, become rivers racing down stems
to flush roots away from native soil, then float off
toward great international rivers, immense iconic oceans
to farthest reaches of the planet
where humans and creatures can still walk
without feet or hooves disappearing.

Caution*

In fall, on a New York coastal island,
    trees have turned
        sunlit yellow, blood orange,
        beefy red.
But, clear among them, a tall, wide vine of
        exotic woodland ivy
    outshouts them all
        in imperial purple, nursery pink,
        iceberg-white,
        bituminous black.

Moving too close
        could be inviting
        harm.

The innocent-appearing vine
completely hides the skeleton
        of a white birch tree
        it has   strangled.

Shaped like valentines, the ivy
    leaves tightly overlap
  to block the sun out
      for the birch
  assuring death.

    Leaves' arteries and veins
      mimic those of the human heart,
      but they're heartless,
        poisoning
    the skin
        with a burning rash
  pus
      that oozes out
  for days, weeks…

  All from a human touch
    as light
      as an
    infant's
      finger.

*Another version of "Rash".

Bob's Excellent New York Visit, 1999

Ignoring speed signs, a midnight Niagara
blows through the city, explodes
windows, pounds ledges, cascades
to the streets, unloads on taxis and truckers,
flushes hookers and homeless from doorways,
sucks me out of bed into the roar of a movie monster
hell-bent on tearing Manhattan apart.
Sink and rise, swallow and snort, engine oil
filling my ears, pooch piss stinging my eyes,
traffic lights bubbling green.
I'm caught in a swirl that swells to the East River,
boils out to the harbor, to the freighters rocking,
liners blocking the channels.
Bruised, choked, a drowning Ahab, I cling
to a buoy that clangs for my life, ride a rolling surge
under Brooklyn Bridge to a flooded Times Square.
A Crusoe in pajamas, I slosh my way
to a traffic island, my eyes into wind,
barely see the faded lights
spelling headlines in motion:

    HURRICANE FLOYD EATS THE APPLE!

Joanie:
(But Not on the Lips)

She's fish-tailing thru the mall, anxious;
twenty minutes late for our date again.
She'll appreciate a kiss on the cheek.
>Way back in '58, rave reviews for her
>B'way debut, left my beautiful bride
>alone in New York.
Me, making docufilms overseas for weeks
and months. And the sloe-eyed foreign
ladies were seductive.

>Tensions grew after every flight,
>but never a fight. Maybe a baby?
>Paula had us both giggling, but still
sleeping in separate worlds. American bucks,
a Mexican judge, and "You are divor-ced!"

>Tonight, on a date, in our favorite
>deli-café, she speaks to the waiter:
"Wild Salmon; is it legally caught? The Crab,
was it flash-frozen quickly? Your Rare Roast
>Beef isn't bloody is it?"

>Quirks that drove us up walls, now

>produce grins. Neither remarried,
>but partnered in growing our daughter,
we have sidestepped the love game, evolved into
friends, in a free-form, unlicensed, family unit.

>Just not on the lips anymore.

Hooked

Impossible I could kill
a thing on wings or legs
but when the hook is set
the rod bent
and a string of line
binds me to a fish
I rapidly transform
to hunter-killer
in the surf.

My nerves, muscles, cells
all jam into a single determined mode
to extract the silent-running swimmer.

Its scaled white belly
touches water's edge, then darts away
in frantic splashes, searching out
a deeper place to shake its jaw
break the bond, leave me
bent on the beach
unnerved and cheated.

But I pull on the rod
wind on the reel
and out of the splashing water it leaps,
heavy, long as arm,
striped in shining silver and black.

It flops about, thumping on sand,
disgorging its food,
gills pumping in rhythms like our own.

Slowly, slowly, life escapes
this Atlantic striped bass.
I try to avoid the growing feeling
that I'm the one who's been hooked.

A Pair of Hooves

In a hollow
torn from the dunes
by ancient tides:
a young doe asleep.

A crunch on sand
and she leaps awake
trembling on furred legs
ready to bound away.

But her velvet face
and black/brown eyes
lead me to Leah
backstage at fifteen
lifting the leaves of her
wood sprite costume
smiling me down
to her cloven hooves.

The doe snorts
sprints up a sand hill
into a stand
of young pines
as Leah sheds her foliage
down to bare feet
on the darkened stage
where we first filled
the spaces
we'd only heard of.

Ship of Sand

Sky blue
turns sickening gray
and ocean blackens.
Winds attack
from north and east,
duneside homes rattle, shiver,
windows implode, our roof tears loose,
sails like a Frisbee giant; shears off chimneys,
slams with a crunch
on the clapboard church, leaves oiled wood floors
and folding chairs underwater.
This ship-of-sand island besieged
like an ocean liner aground,
motor launches and clammers and dories evacuating
all but die-hard denizens.

The shell of our house
now lifted away and dropped with a crush
on a cluster of pines. Under the bare wooded platform,
a group stands shoulder to shoulder
recounting the heartbreak,
waiting for the monster to sate its hunger,
move out to sea.

Treading the tide, drooling on waves,
waiting through night
for morning to gather its winds from double directions
to roar, thunder and race to attack
the all-but-abandoned Ship of Sand again.
Then, slowly, fade, whistle away by noon,
as Coast Guard and a horde of civilian craft
approach on the bay:
they look like air force photos
of a miniature Normandy invasion.

Epitaph

Poet still dying down here.

Holding on for a last look at love
in your faces, bouquets,
and
tears,
seeping
through sod.

Remember me for this:

On the moon, I waved hello to daylight,
spun the dust of stars
into rain.
Watched sun suck blood
from
silk petal flowers.
Saw elephants swim
in drops
of olive oil,
and lions eat roses
in an
arctic storm.

Private First Class

Flown in
to swirling eddies of oil
black grass and green air.

All afternoon to evening
she waits, full-pack, for orders.

An exploding bouquet of steel
erases birds in flight, fires helmets
through sharded windows
drops her body in terminal shock.

Far from her favorite stars over
Maine, Pfc. (name withheld)
is cradled by marines behind a tank
as her breathing comes to a stop.

Bagged, zipped, returned.
Never again
a New England turning of leaves.

At the Crash Site Near Nagoya

Miyoki, my dear wife,

If this note is in your hands, it will be that I have died.
We are rolling side to side in the night sky, somewhere
east of Kyoto, the crew searching the storm for a place
to land. Use of phones is forbidden, but in the dim light
lining the aisle, I hope there is time for truths I must
tell. To assure you that on the night you question, I did
not share your sister's bed. I sat in shadow in her room
until sunlight warmed the floor, then I walked away.
I cannot explain my conduct more, please make your
peace with her, she had no fault. The other truth is that
I lied to you about our lack of children. Due to your
health conditions, I could not risk the gaining of a child,
but losing you. Smiling falsely, I said I wanted none, but
the doubt in your eyes still haunts my mind. We must be
nearing the mountains, they call crash-land positions.
I will now fold this note into the silver smoking case
you gave me for my forty-second birthday. If it comes
to you, Myoki, place it on the red lacquered table beside
your bridal photo.

Your loving husband,

Takashi

94

I Want to Go in Motion

not lingering horizontal
or propped up in a winter chair
but jogging
hooded
in fall rain
a lightning rush of heartbeats
a slow final blink
the view is trees
shining in their wind colors.

Or walking on new stones
green with algae
a clot moves
a stagger
a splash.

Driving through a storm
seized in a tornado
slammed
whirled.

Blown anonymous.

Appendix

Alternative Version of **"Project in Process"**

Firstborn

The pregnant mound quivers,
grunts and moans
from the earthbound Momma,
stares and sweat
from the sky-high Dad.

Deep inside, The Project tilts,
prepares for launch
is pushed down hard,
squeezed out dripping
like a parboiled chicken.
Fuel line trailing
from a burned-out Momma,
Daddy in a heap on green tile floor.

Upside down and whacked on the bottom,
the Thing inflates,
turns purple-red.
Transmogrifies
to a wriggling, squint-eyed
all-out Paula
with a vision of power,
a shower of pizzazz.

ABOUT THE AUTHOR

Boston born, Bob Foster was an actor, director, writer, and producer in theatre, television, and documentary films before a life-long attraction to poetry took hold.

After graduating from the Bishop-Lee School of the Theatre (Boston), he played about one hundred roles and directed plays in summer stock and regional theatres throughout New England. While studying at the American Theatre Wing in New York, he landed a featured role in the Katharine Hepburn revival of Shakespeare's *As You Like It* on Broadway, running for two seasons including a nationwide tour.

Later, he directed many television productions, including dramas at ABC and NBC in New York. Then Bob turned to documentary films: writing, directing, and producing, mainly for the U.S. Information Agency and NASA, to be shown on television worldwide.

Finally, the drive to write poetry overwhelmed any thoughts of retirement. In the past decade he has studied with Suzanne Lummis (UCLA), Cecilia Woloch (Idyllwild Summer Poetry), Sarah Maclay (Beyond Baroque in Venice, California), and at the Midnight Special Workshop (Santa Monica).

Bob has been a featured reader of his poems in bookstores, libraries, and cafés throughout Southern California. And his work has been published in many journals, including *Spillway, Aethelon, Rose, Wordtrack,* and *Creative Living.*